EXPLORING SPACE

GALAXIES

WRITTEN BY E.C. ANDREWS

Gareth Stevens PUBLISHING

Please visit our website, www.garethstevens.com. For a free color catalog of all our high-quality books, call toll free 1-800-542-2595 or fax 1-877-542-2596.

Published in 2025 by
Gareth Stevens Publishing
2544 Clinton St.
Buffalo, NY 14224

Written by:
E.C. Andrews

Edited by:
Noah Leatherland

Designed by:
Ker Ker Lee

Cataloging-in-Publication Data

Names: Andrews, E.C.
Title: Galaxies / E.C. Andrews.
Description: Buffalo, NY : Gareth Stevens Publishing, 2025. | Series: Exploring space | Includes glossary and index.
Identifiers: ISBN 9781482468632 (pbk.) | ISBN 9781482468649 (library bound) | ISBN 9781482468656 (ebook)
Subjects: LCSH: Galaxies--Juvenile literature.
Classification: LCC QB857.3 A537 2025 | DDC 523.1'12--dc23

Printed in the United States of America

CPSIA compliance information: Batch #CW25GS: For further information contact Gareth Stevens at 1-800-542-2595.

Find us on

Photo Credits – Images are courtesy of Shutterstock.com. With thanks to Getty Images, Thinkstock Photo and iStockphoto.

Recurring images – Vector Tradition. Cover – Triff. 2–3 – Triffi. 4–5 – Dima Zel, Triff. 6–7 – Wolfgang Kloehr, Roupplar, NASA images, M.Aurelius. 8–9 – Helioscribe, Vadim Sadovski. 10–11 – Triff, MaraQu. 12–13 – Ammit Jack, Withan Tor. 14–15 – Nova Dawn Astrophotography, CC BY-SA 4.0 <https://creativecommons.org/licenses/by-sa/4.0>, via Wikimedia Commons, ESO/Bayerischer Rundfunk, CC BY 4.0 <https://creativecommons.org/licenses/by/4.0>, via Wikimedia Commons. 16–17 – Vadim Sadovski, buradaki. 18–19 – Malll Themd, REDPIXEL.PL. 20–21 – Yuriy Kulik, Potapovpaladin, AustralianCamera. 22–23 – Triff, 24K-Production.

CONTENTS

Words that look like this can be found in the glossary on page 24.

WHAT IS SPACE?

Space is what scientists call the mysterious place outside Earth. A lot of scientists think that space is infinite. This means it goes on forever. However, nobody knows this for sure.

Most living things need a gas called oxygen to survive. There is no oxygen in space. Many scientists do not think there are living things anywhere outside of Earth. However, there are plenty of other fascinating things in space.

WHAT ARE GALAXIES?

Galaxies are huge collections of dust, gas, and stars. Galaxies come in different shapes and sizes. Some galaxies are shaped like spirals. Galaxies that are shaped like ovals are called elliptical galaxies.

SPIRAL GALAXY

IRREGULAR GALAXY

ELLIPTICAL GALAXY

Galaxies with unique shapes are called irregular galaxies.

There are so many galaxies in space that scientists cannot count them all. Some scientists think there may be over two trillion! There are probably a lot more that have not been discovered yet.

GRAVITY

On Earth, gravity is the force that pulls you towards the ground. Gravity is the reason things fall to the floor when you drop them. Without gravity, everything on Earth would float away.

In space, the gravity from larger objects, such as planets, pulls smaller objects towards them. This is called gravitational pull. Galaxies are created and held together by gravity.

HOW ARE GALAXIES CREATED?

Galaxies are thought to begin as much smaller clouds of stars and dust swirling around in space. Sometimes, the gravity from the stars begins pulling smaller objects towards them.

These small clouds sometimes get pulled towards one another by the gravitational pull of the stars. When they hit each other, they can become linked together. This forms a galaxy.

THE MILKY WAY

When you look into the night sky, you may see something that looks like a trail of glitter. You are probably looking at the Milky Way. This is the galaxy that Earth is in.

THE SUN

The Milky Way is a spiral galaxy. That trail of glitter is part of the spiral.

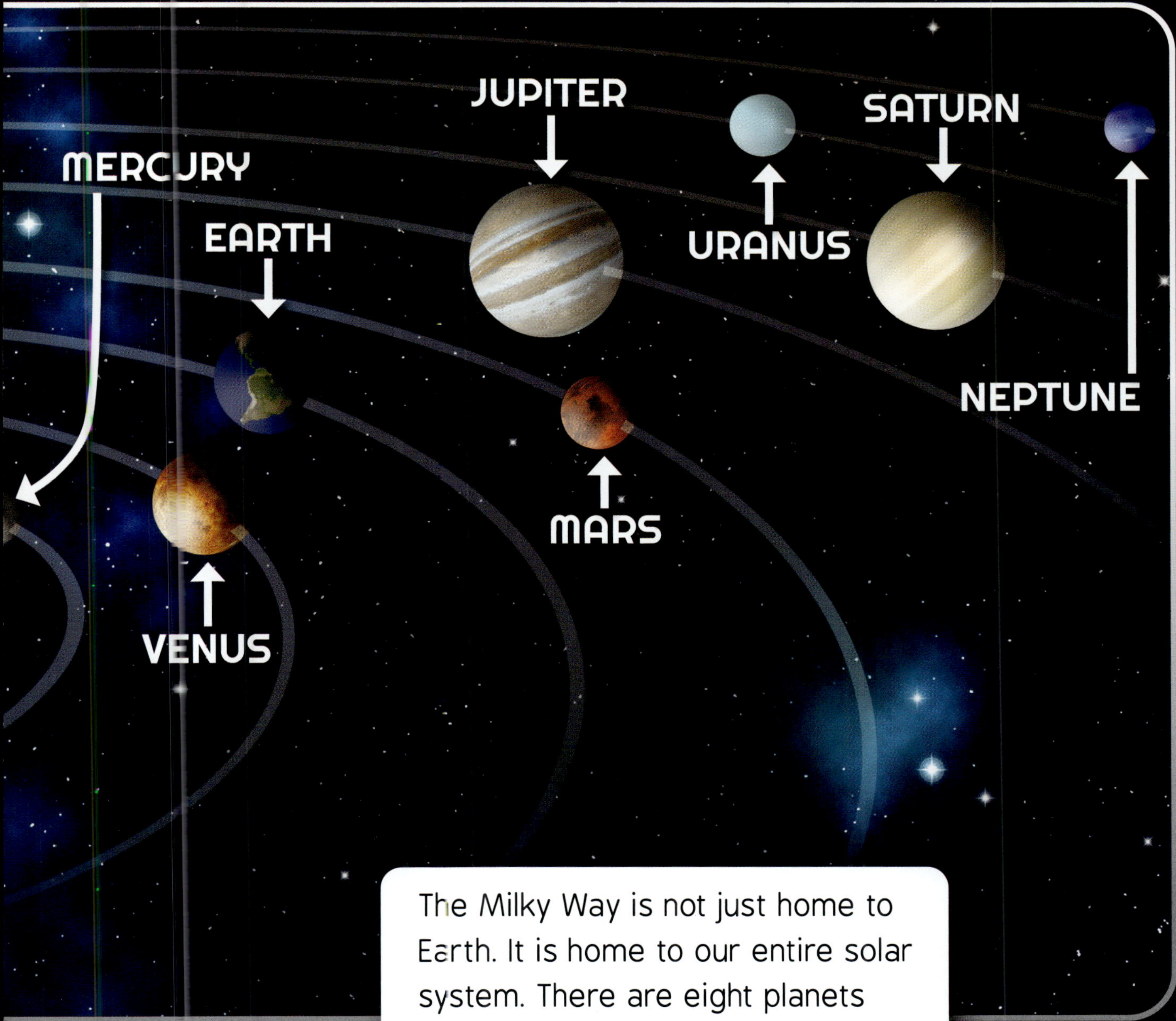

The Milky Way is not just home to Earth. It is home to our entire solar system. There are eight planets in our solar system. They all orbit around a star. This star is our sun.

STARS

The Milky Way is surrounded by lots of twinkling stars. Some stars may look very bright. However, all those stars are trillions of miles away. Up close, stars are giant balls of burning gas.

Stars are made when clouds of dust and very cold gas clump together. This can create a stronger gravitational pull. Sometimes, these clouds of gas and dust collapse under the force of the gravity. This creates stars.

There are more than 100 billion stars in the Milky way alone.

DARK MATTER

In galaxies, gravitational pull does not just come from stars. It also comes from dark matter. Ordinary matter makes up everything around you. However, dark matter is extremely mysterious.

Dark matter cannot be seen or touched. Not much is known about dark matter. Scientists do not fully understand it. However, we know that its gravitational pull is important when it comes to holding galaxies together.

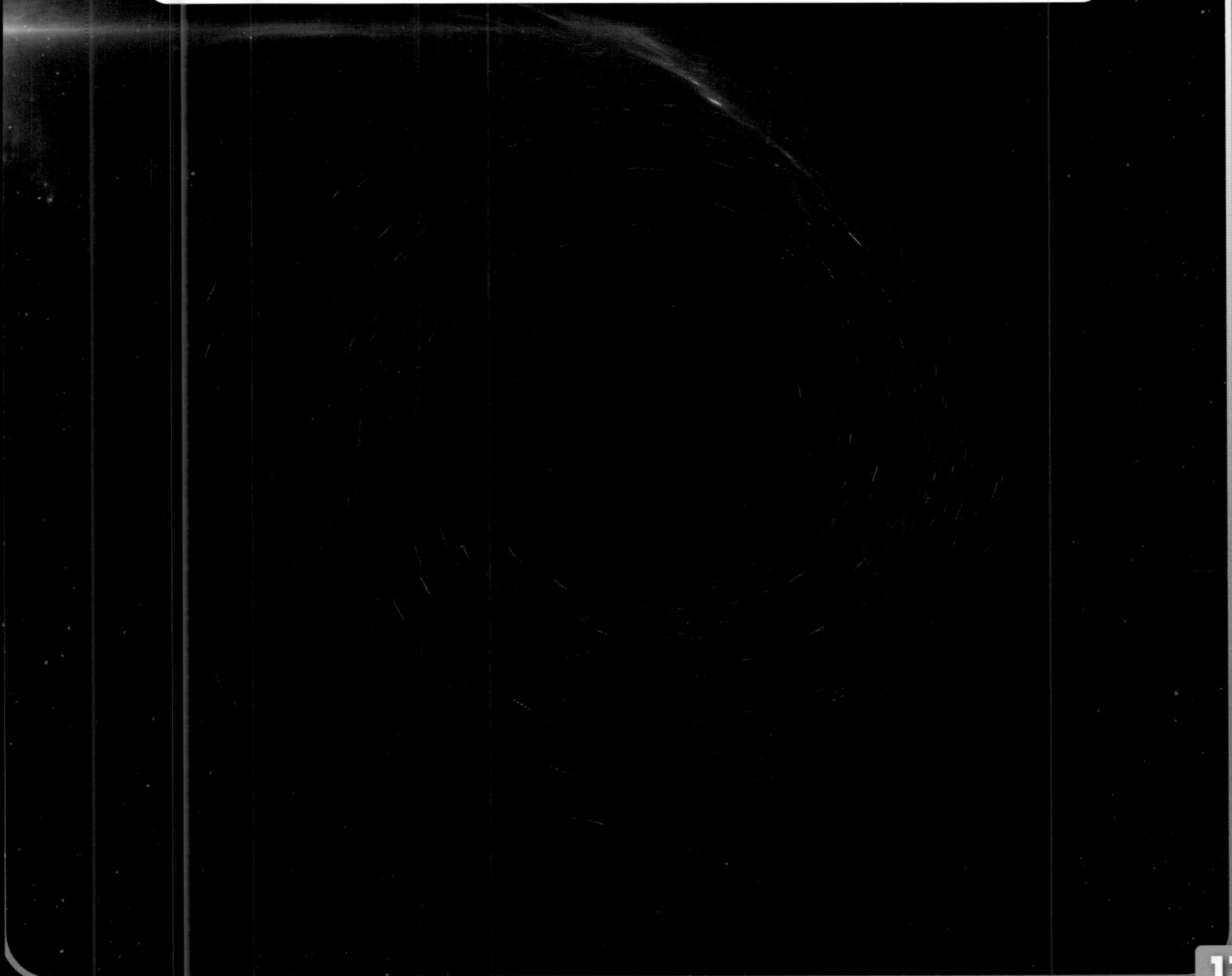

BLACK HOLES

In the middle of a lot of galaxies, there is something called a black hole. There is a black hole in the middle of the Milky Way called Sagittarius A*.

Black holes are also very mysterious. They do not give off or reflect any light. This makes them invisible to telescopes. However, the gravitational pull of black holes can cause stars to orbit around them.

CONSTELLATIONS

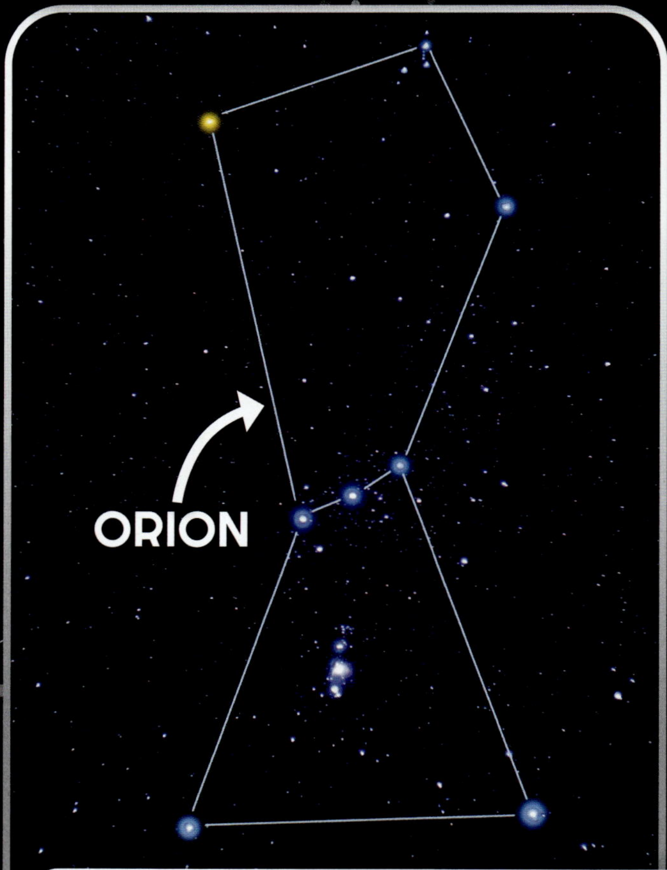

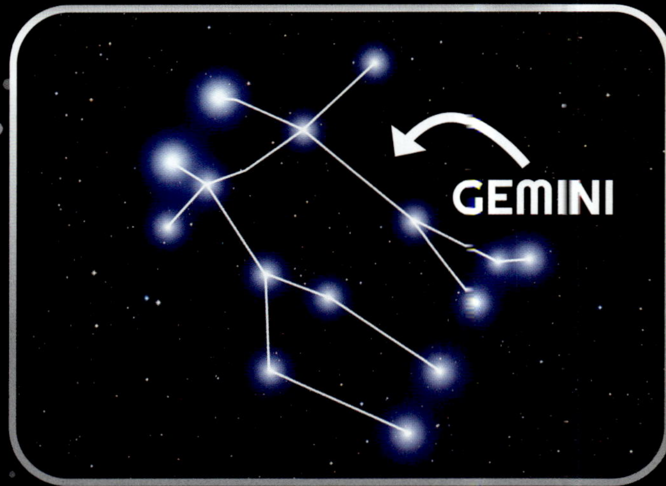

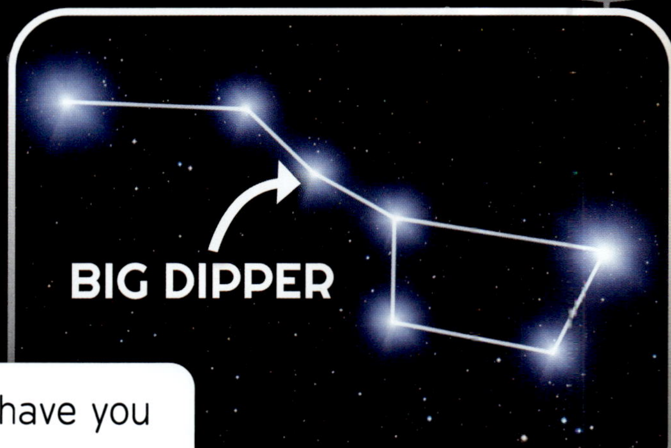

When you look up into the night sky, have you ever noticed patterns in the stars? You may be looking at a constellation. In ancient times, people such as the Greeks, Romans, and Babylonians named these patterns.

There are 88 known constellations in the sky.

Many constellations are named after famous people and creatures from mythology. The Babylonians used patterns in the stars to create star signs. Everyone has a star sign based on when they were born.

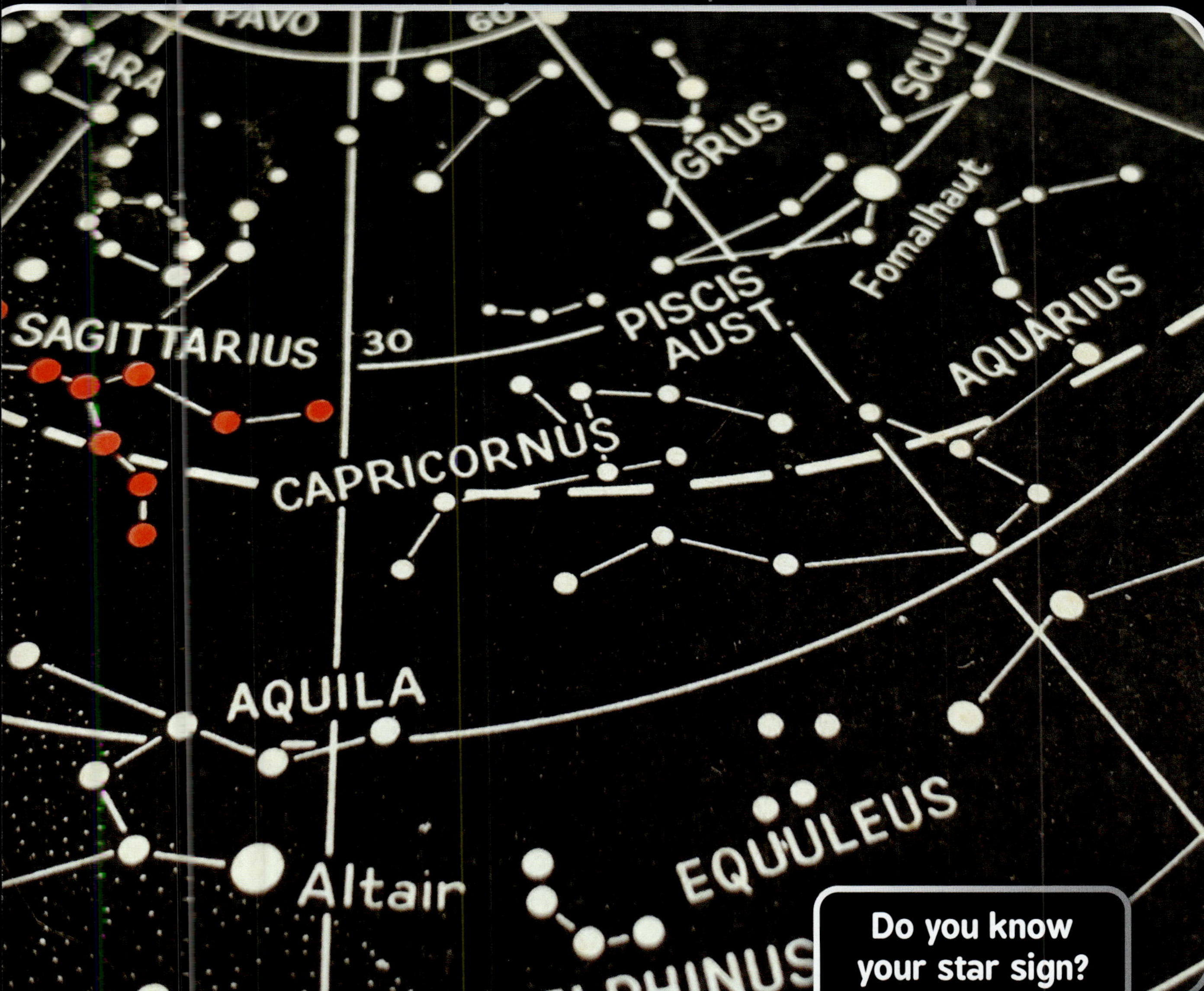

Do you know your star sign?

Galaxies are home to many different things, from planets and stars to dark matter and black holes. There is so much to discover. What part of the galaxy do you want to learn more about?

There are more galaxies in space than can possibly be counted. So far, the Milky Way is the only galaxy that scientists know to have living things in it. Those living things are all on Earth.

Do you think there may be living things somewhere else in space?

GLOSSARY

ancient	belonging to the very distant past
gas	a thing that is like air, which spreads out to fill any space available
mythology	a collection of old stories that belong to a group of people
orbit	to move around a star or planet in a curved path
reflect	to bounce back light, heat, or sound
survive	to stay alive
unique	one of a kind or very rare

INDEX